# REEL

Reel

FIRST EDITION


Printed in the United States of America
ISBN 979·8·9897084·3·7

COVER ARTWORK
Stills from Maya Deren's unfinished short film "Ensemble for Somnambulists", 1951.

DESIGN ≈ SEVY PEREZ
Text in Brandon Grotesque & Adobe Caslon Pro

*This book is published by the*
Cleveland State University Poetry Center
csupoetrycenter.com
2121 Euclid Avenue, Cleveland, Ohio 44115-2214

A CATALOG RECORD FOR THIS TITLE IS
AVAILABLE FROM THE LIBRARY OF CONGRESS

# REEL

COLLEEN O'BRIEN

*for Brandon & Ezra*

# I

## Seeing

To still to cold
lucidity, to absolute,
the pulsing

visual field: arrest
the tachycardic
eye's pulse, eye

a clear fish
egg, iris and vitreous
humor colorless:

to sear
all sterile
by isothermal

chill: to take
all in—styptic
and antivolatile.

## *For Now*

the infant's eyes' unheimlich
automatic motion

open asleep in the foremilk
of human cognition,

in blank concatenation:
rampant rebus minus

meaning: a color-
shallow surface

blindly doubling
the ceiling

fan blades' turning

## Scatter

ash
largesse
plot &

the terrified

brain of a woman

question: what are things that

## *Habilitate*

I didn't mean to be at this party

first I was alone

I had all these old dresses and was trying to find one
he hadn't seen

the party grew larger

it was after all a party not just people

a high number now there must
be preferences

I was excited though to be at a party

I would tell my friends oh yeah I
was just at this party

I tried to find a dress that wouldn't hurt his feelings

this one my dad bought me when I was twenty

I was paranoid the lady at the store
thought we were dating

I envy now what then I

stop that it's wrong

it can help though
at this kind of party

I had this new dress but he had seen it

I had all these problems with my hands
the doctor said I should

be ashamed

I gathered my things and moved away
from preferences

I kept looking at them

I chose a dress he'd know I wasn't wearing

for that reason

## *Midas*

I sit here in ass's ears
through which no human
language passes,

only the four-tone scale
of all mammalia: relief
and coming relief, pain

and coming pain. The notes
sound nearly always
in isolation,

occasionally in ligated
but still distinct dyads.
Every hour I forget

more of the sapiens
mouth, even its ordinary
virtuosity,

and every hour I am
more afraid to speak.

## *The Interpretation of Dreams*

All the stage is
bearded like a pard, is

justice in her.

All the quarrel, his satchel,
hose with eyes

severe.

        A ballad to her.

All the wide is
creeping like her

beard of formal
cut,

the cannon's mouth,

sans teeth.

Big manly pard, sudden
furnace his

big manly
ballad.

Eyebrow.

His shrunk.

Last strange of
all a world

too wide.

## *Ruined Lion*

Mane of moss,
maw simplified to toothless

shrunken gums. Demoted to a phylum
worse, some white-eyed

sucking worm. His mother burst
with none to nurse, she's

melted to her throne.
Has crying done

that to her face? What turns
stone to loam?

## ***Because We Want***

it there, we put
it there

our wanting it
is it:

        father
        lover
lastly
        genre

a variation on refrain

        (smell of sex,
        drinking
        with children in the house)

because we put it there

        (how we
        all stayed friends)

every borrowing

drags along with it
    the whole

we put it there because

please here

# II

## *Molly*

o rocks! un

        faithful
Penny in rank
bedsheets, reading dirty books to ferry all

ye blaze, ye boil
        ing souls over the white fat foaming

oash, one waving
        luscious arm, bare from her

window, seen
by whom? that scrap

        of morning

mail, the privy under bed
        awaiting her

Hellenic stream,
        her instrument

beneath, untuned
                        piano where she ulu

lates, undoes
        the day's loom

work again,
        again she says,

        against
the soldier's youth

ful wall,
        and da, and da
rkness lit by moon, all
moonsday, met him

        wild
centrifuge rose

en bloom

## Ergo Ego

all ends and
                    I am profoundly
I can bear to say
                    unafraid of death
          this only
                    because I do not
                    believe in death
in other languages          certainly not
                                        my own

***Michael Finnegan***

re
begin

afoul
of all

intimacy

*

forgave all debts,
grand gestures, etc.

*

from here there shall can

only more no less

*

i was sober six years and six months and

*

bursting can spits

like in the
ad mists

her screen-lit face she

wipes her chin

*

re be
gin your ún

intén

did what
’s the french for

cry for

*

write sober edit sober makes john
imagine decomposing women in
the steam

*goddamn, girlflesh*
*stay on!*

*

the choice does seem lose one
or other mind

or matter

*

begin can
re can

know an old man named

poor

## *Coming Down*

Aphorisms on stone benches
Neon in a gallery

Who was that was that

gone in long

return

thick with fantasy

a concentrated color rivuleting into water
          filamenting

into water

what if we took no photos

          eye contact with a child is like

what if we made no videos what

if the

were the art

the fingerprint what if

I were as neon sober as
aphoristic sober as what

not to be

small but larger

plastic pearls on a woman's dress if you remembered
plastic pearls on a woman's dress

Aphorisms in new asphalt
Neon against collision

who was

## *Fuel*

And I am the downed tree
        and the thriving sorrel

the calcite
        logarithmic spiral
shell and the gum

creature
oozing and perishing inside

My live corpse feeds
        the frothing ever breeding

        my multiplying

petrifies

## *Bethlehem*

i

Speak back

to speak back
idiotically

ii

o but not idiot:

subordinate

A tale told by
subordinate

full of sound

iii

Speak back

*(ba dá, da dá, da dá, da dá)*
And dust is for a time

iv

in wrist to hydrate me in childbirth (vomited my last meal, mug of milk warmed in microwave, two a.m. winter dark kitchen; now blood pressure low)

v

Speak back
to speak back
geriatrically

till the end came
in the end came

close of a long day

vi

o but no

you tell her

no. no. no. no. no-no-no-no
no. no. no. no. no-no-no-no
no. no. no. no. no.

her love belongs to me

vii

patronym, the Ní
shortened form of Iníon Uí:

daughter of descendant of

viii

That's right, say my name

ix

Cold surface
*Iron is iron till it is rust*
Don't hurt me now, don't hurt me now

x

what followed wasn't, now you see
a star

at all a star wasn't

what you see you
followed

xi

back amniotically
into the lukewarm tub
shreds of clotted blood and meconium

back where was seized
body before name

xii

speak you never speak

## *Wind Turns Rain*

wind turns rain and all
          shatters lightly

          but does
not separate

a dripping geometric
          darkness lids

          the moving

grows

behind the rain the
hill road we go

          closer farther

# III

## Genealogy

There are those who wake
and rightly wrongly think

*most of what my parents said*
*was close to right and close to good*

Then there are those who wake
in on/outside the joke:

*the wolves were wolves*
*that stuff we drank was blood*

Always the twain shall meet,
consort and procreate,
divorce or die or not.

Then there are those who wake
two-mouthed

*what blood stuff was said most*
*close to wolves we drank*
*my parents were what was*

## *Winter*

The counting time the toys
the children eat their
candy wrappers every
where and we

in robes & spectacles
exchange mementos
mori this year's load the
next year's *can we*

*toss this please?* the strain
the lotions human
feet disfigured in
their shoes but too:

young bodies making un
intended life furor
sanandi in the cold
so why do old

men stand at windows
in the dark? it melts!
old man it turns
back toward

the sun we fill until
we flood until
we drain until
the cold again drink drink

## *Moving*

i.

sapling's training
tube cracked & curved away
from the sapling

thought to reach out to

gaudy sun rising
behind old dead
water park

doubled then,
a Venn
in the west bus window

haystack sky mit frost don't
photograph it babe i'll only

let you down

ii.

increasingly a currency
i can't use

1 cup loose pearls provide provide

x's & v's the power
lines & vinyl siding tomb
shaped signs on lawns WE

ARE SECURE

iii.

it's true i feel abandoned Mattress
Warehouse true i feel abandoned
Aspen Dental young

women in sunglasses captioned
*start your career*

Natural Stone Right Here

iv.

i like old cities where the art's been dead for decades
i like old photos full of people holding still
i like to sit pretending time must be a circle
i like to laugh at those who know that time's a line

i like it when you say you're sorry
as if to say it's true all those things happened

metal behind the trees becomes a wall of light
the sun i mean the bus moves and it's trees

## *Envy*

woke denying
the dream

didn't count
your blessings, bitch,

one Ur text
message none

would call a [find a
foreign word]

besides you
love her

bedside you
aren't that

[leave this blank] not

even for a second

honeymoon
suite ladies

be gentle
men my

ego's in your hands

## *The After-Man*

wants ~~an art that~~

a that which

exceeds ~~calculation and~~

wants

~~abrogation of~~
a that with which

to reset
~~the hands of the~~

the heads of the
clock

wants

at zero

a clock which

wants

to reset
with

hands ~~which~~
but

breaking with the past [strikethru]

is actually ~~forgetting~~

repeating

the ~~sublime is~~
that which

~~is wanted~~ exceeds

breaking

## *Judith Butler*

through the many mattresses she
felt the tiny, adamant pea

and couldn't sleep

and picked a thread,
another thread, tore up

a boll
of fluffy stuff,

tempest
of feathers and frivolité,

of knotted lace,
the shuttles mummying

stout thread, she found
the cache of silicone

and wrinkled dugs
and dug

on down—confessed
(they begged) it's just

a little better for the man—

and when
she had it in her hand,

the dived-for bit
of oyster grit,

the mattresses a shameless
mess,

she slid it neatly in
her ring

and went to wake
the castle up.

# IV

## *Rich White Guy Gets What He Wants*

EXTRA EXTRA

## *Saturn*

Red throat,
expel today
the substitute:
the stone. The boy

is back from
underground
today. The boy
has grown.

The undigested
breach in yellow
glory from my
mouth. Then blast

me nine days'
anvil flight away
from wide
wayed earth.

## *In the Democracy*

My father went to the mirror
every morning half naked
and scraped cream
from his beard. He flexed
both biceps, blue
plastic razor puny
in his fist. His face
half cream, half red
and clean, he made
a beast-face to make
me shriek laughing.
He believed
that he was joking.

## ***Bathers by a River***
*after Matisse*

i.

Here, in the breath white
light the long necked
girl, from a moment

when logic, form,
and organ met—
supple reaching neck—

and eye confirmed
what mind prescribed.

ii.

Black gravity
and gray vibration:
Electrons or
their likelihood.

Green where his mind changed.
Previous green in
simultaneous pink.

iii.

Eight years
for a long moment.

Given the chance
he'd change it.
Reeds pile like Sunday palms
on the moment.

iv.

He found her body
at last like a tree
in the reeds.
Blackline growth
up the cloven legs
and buttocks

as in that miniature
Cézanne he called moral,
black wet locks
coiled like proteins.

## *Child Is Father*

We are farther post-reason and faster entropic,
make more of our movements and less of our masses.

We matter as physics. Our matter's less ethics.
Without them we're moral as moons and we orbit

no center. We make a mathematics
that roots in a stillness less stable than zero.

We matter as ether, no-telos our telos,
and stake your ascendance with flags of our absence.

## *Consolation to a Friend*

You had more talent than he did.
His luck came younger.
World knows the way that goes:
luck, hunger, and luck-hunger.

Or was the difference inside?
One must have a mind of summer
to get the grapes the rest of us
are jumping under,

which obviously are ripe
but won't fill one forever.

## *All*

her life with
you in the slow
car livid

her life with
you in the slow
car livid

this year
a knife

*

tendons in the meat

thick plastic lashes harmless
things

*

you were hurt

i was hurt too

i was eight

*

a political party of everyone
who is eight

*

on the counter
in the expensive
kitchen a pill

name brand duh

you in slow
time livid

you in your
literal toy helmet

# V

## *Poem for Your Walk This Morning*

With the rabbit
in the backyard headlights last night
something long-tailed

muskrat possum

someone
would know: I don't,
said Larkin & my love & I now
say it often.

With the poet
in the background things take
untrustworthy

singularity radiance

no one
would see: I don't
if put near other
people often.

What's it for
then?     Solitary
non confinement

## *He's in Bed*

some dancers'
nerves are dead this

is our fault

school is hell

*

the child is
not bad

the teacher is
not bad

knowledge is

*

legs in net
strong because

ribbons all
the way
up

*

the child is telling the truth
the child's tears tell the truth

the teacher deserves love
the teacher's nerves are dead

*

fuck that bitch I didn't say

what's wrong

my husband said

*

the child wants to know
what

you don't

## *Postcard*

Dear Sis, We've been in Prague two weeks almost
exactly to the hour, and I admit
I'm counting time that way: I'm worrying
about its passing, therefore wasting it.
Bohuzel, they say, or "to God's sorrow,"
I've tried to learn the language. Dobrý den.
I've read Kundera (one). It's Europe, so
I told myself I could drink wine again.
I thought I wept for Kafka. Probably
I wept because I've fought so much with B.
Great art's a funicular ride up to
self-centeredness, for dilettantes like me.
But blah blah blah. I'm tired. I'm probably drunk.
When I get home I'll love this place, I think.

## *Old Notes*

rereading old notes I take
a semicolon for a lowercase *i*

; confuse *i*
with a kind

of notational fulcrum ; take
a hybrid

a stacked
stop and go

for a kind
of notational fiction

[stop stop] many centuries'
pondering [stop stop]

"note thinks therefore
note is" [stop go]

then typing drop
the *e* on *note*

“not thinks therefore . . .”

it’s not
like *me* to lowercase

whimsically [stop go] it’s not
like *me* to game italics, splash

[quote quote] and such

about, say *o*

paren
but then,
what *is* it like?

paren

*look at me* [go]

## This Time

Which is it
then? Are you

a naked woman
or a woman

wearing clothes?
The truth,

Madam.

## *Reel*

A reel is a dance,
a spool,
and a fall fast and straight
at the wall.

To reel and to fall make a cross
like to rise and to sail.
To bow makes a compass
to draw on the floor.

A draw is a truce.
The fall ends the year.
A headstone's a tooth
in the mouth of the earth.

Truth is a word
in the mouth
and a spool in the maze
in the myth.

## *Those Are Pearls*

Row row row your boat, gently down the stream your boat, merrily merrily mer your boat: Life is but a dream your boat

Gently down the stream your boat, gentilly downily row your boat, gently but the stream your boat: Life is merrily row your boat

Row is but a dream your boatily, gently but a row your boatily, row is merrily dream your boatily, merrily but a merrily boatily

Life is but a dream your boat: Life is but the stream your boat: Life is down the stream your boat: Gently but the stream your boat

Gently down the stream your merrily, row row row your merrily, gently down the streamily merrily, row is but a row your merrily

Merrily merrily merrily merrily, merrily merrily merrily merrily, merrily merrily merrily merrily, merrily merrily merrily merrily

## Notes

The poem "Bethlehem" borrows and distorts lines from Shakespeare's "Macbeth," Marianne Moore's "In Distrust of Merits," Samuel Beckett's "Rockaby," The Zombies' "Tell Her No," Ghostface Killah's remix of Amy Winehouse's "You Know I'm No Good," and T. S. Eliot's *The Waste Land*.

The poem "The After-Man" engages language and concepts from the headnote to Jean-François Lyotard in *The Norton Anthology of Theory and Criticism*, eds. Vincent B. Leitch, et al.

## Acknowledgments

Grateful acknowledgement is made to the editors of the following journals, who first published versions of these poems: *Another Chicago Magazine*, *Beloit Poetry Journal*, *CutBank*, *Denver Quarterly*, *DIAGRAM*, *Fence*, *Interim*, *The Journal*, *Kenyon Review Online*, *Newfound*, *Poetry Northwest*, *RHINO*, *The Volta*, *West Branch*, *Witness*; and to the editors of New Michigan Press, who published versions of some of them in my chapbook, *Spool in the Maze*.

## RECENT CLEVELAND STATE UNIVERSITY POETRY CENTER PUBLICATIONS

***edited by Caryl Pagel & Hilary Plum***

**POETRY**

*Mechanical Bull* by Rennie Ament

*World'd Too Much: The Selected Poetry of Russell Atkins*
ed. Kevin Prufer and Robert E. McDonough

*Advantages of Being Evergreen* by Oliver Baez Bendorf

*The Devil's Workshop* by Xavier Cavazos

*Ordinary Entanglement* by Melissa Dickey

*Dream Boat* by Shelley Feller

*My Fault* by Leora Fridman

*Orient* by Nicholas Gulig

*Twice There Was A Country* by Alen Hamza

*Age of Glass* by Anna Maria Hong

*outside voices, please* by Valerie Hsiung

*In One Form to Find Another* by Jane Lewty

*50 Water Dreams* by Siwar Masannat

*Mule: 10th Anniversary Edition* by Shane McCrae

*daughterrarium* by Sheila McMullin

*The Bees Make Money in the Lion* by Lo Kwa Mei-en

*Residuum* by Martin Rock

*Festival* by Broc Rossell

*Sun Cycle* by Anne Lesley Selcer

*Arena* by Lauren Shapiro

*Bottle the Bottles the Bottles the Bottles* by Lee Upton

*Innocence* by Michael Joseph Walsh

*No Doubt I Will Return A Different Man* by Tobias Wray

**ESSAYS**

*I want to start by saying* by Samuel Ace

*I Liked You Better Before I Knew You So Well*
by James Allen Hall

*A Bestiary* by Lily Hoang

*Codependence* by Amy Long

*Telephone: Essays in Two Voices*
by Brenda Miller and Julie Marie Wade

*The Leftovers* by Shaelyn Smith

**TRANSLATIONS**

*No One Knows Their Blood Type* by Maya Abu Al-Hayyat,
translated by Hazem Jamjoum

*Almost Obscene* by Raúl Gómez Jattin,
translated by Katherine M. Hedeen and Olivia Lott

*Scorpionic Sun* by Mohammed Khaïr-Eddine,
translated by Conor Bracken

*I Burned at the Feast: Selected Poems of Arseny Tarkovsky*,
translated by Philip Metres and Dimitri Psurtsev

***for a complete list of titles visit CSUPoetryCenter.com***